THE SECRET SCION

Adegboye Samuel

TABLE OF CONTENTS

Chapter 1

Confinement

"Philip Bamford!" The matron of Keith mental boys home yelled his name, making his heart skip a beat. He walked really fast down the hallway with his head bent, going towards the direction the voice was calling from. "What have I done this time?" He muttered under his breath. He silently opened the door to Miss Howard's office, head bent, hands clutched behind him.

Why always me, for goodness' sake!

"Philip." A quick smile broke through her face.

"Sit down,"

she said, pointing to the chair in front of her. By the time he settled into the chair, the smile had disappeared.

"You've been here since you were eleven, for allegedly killing your father due to mental disorder. I know you have been anticipating your release from here; which is a good thing. Your ten-year ban from family friends and the outside world is going to be over in a week" By now he was going from being impatient to getting angry. What's up with the suspense ma'am? Just pass the message already.

"I know you really want to be reunited with your family, but... for another five years,

" She continued " your mother will visit you, provided you're well behaved. Your mental health will also be monitored and developed. You can go back to your dormitory now".

"Thank you, ma'am,"

he said as he quietly left her office. He maintains the posture he went in with, but this time, tear drops are slowly crawling down his cheeks. Another five years in this horrible place, after being here ten years already...can it get any better?

"Hey Phil" Terry called out to him.

"Why did that goth call you?".

Philip managed to look up, his face soaked in tears "Extra five years Terry, five years" he said and looked out of the window. Philip, Terry and a few others were the only mentally stable boys in the home. Philip especially was already suffering from a very low self-esteem, but how did he get here in the first place?

Chapter 2

Intentions...

It's a party at Mr. Solomon Bamford's. Philip, their only son had always looked forward to his dad's birthday, because the month coming right after that is his own birthday. So, March and April were always the most exciting times for Philip, until this one. They were the beginning of his tragedy, and often times, he'd ask himself why it had to be the merry times. He would not stop blaming himself for what happened. But he had other people involved in the blame game against him.

The day had started out with his dad in a blue suit and a pair of black shoes. The shoes were the major talking point on that day, you won't say you didn't notice them; they had glittering stones on them. Mrs. Bamford? You should've been there to see her. She looked ten years younger. She was naturally beautiful, but that beauty wouldn't go unnoticed when she appeared in her flowing crimson gown, holding the eleven-year-old Philip by the hand. It was all smiles. Just when Mr. Bamford was about to take the microphone and give a speech, Tim, his closest guard, came close and whispered into his ears. Solomon nodded his head in agreement, dropped the microphone, and headed to his office.

The birthday party took place at their house, but it wasn't just any kind of house, it was a magnificent abode. Philip's father was known for four things; his workaholism, his love for his family, his love for whiskey, and his love for his untrustworthy brother. Yes, untrustworthy. Solomon got to his office and saw his brother, Mike, facing the wall with his hands on his waist.

"Yes Mike, be quick, there are people waiting for me" Solomon said impatiently

"Hey bro!" Mike turned with a smile, picking up two glasses of whiskey and passing one to his brother "Happy birthday to you man"

"Mike" Solomon collected the wine glass but didn't smile "What do you want? You don't do stuff like this, not even on my birthdays, so tell me, what's the catch?"

"Common man!" Mike playfully slapped his brother's shoulder "There's a first time. There's always a first time. But bro," He continued, scratching the side of his head "I need that fifty percent". Solomon stood up slightly annoyed. He downed the content of the wine glass pointed to his brother.

"I knew it. I knew you needed something; that's the reason for the whiskey and all that. Look, I can't give you fifty percent. I have a family, you don't. I wonder what you're using all that money for, at the end of the day, you still launder the company financially. I started this company; I paid your fees - our fees when we were in school. I established you, us! I fought tooth and nail for us to feed, while you made trouble everywhere" By now, Solomon's voice was getting really loud.

"I employed you, and all you do is to come into my office and ask me for fifty percent of a contract I worked for? You must be very funny." He said and stormed out of the office.

"I'm really fed up. I knew he wouldn't give me half of it. Anyways, problem solved". Mike said as he winked at Tim and left the office silently.

Chapter 3

Entrapped Execution

The party was still on with beats blaring out of the speakers. People had eaten and drunk to their fill, and Philip's dad was no exclusion. He was sitting on a chair close to the swimming pool with his jacket off, revealing a white shirt that was tucked in halfway.

"Dad, it's time to go inside" he said, trying to pull his dad to his feet. "Dad, mummy said I shou…" He paused when he noticed his dad bleeding from his nose. "Help! Someone helps" He yelled in his childish voice, but no one heard him. He tried to pull his dad up, but his force wasn't enough. By now, Solomon's mouth was bleeding as well. He tried again, this time, Solomon stood up a little and fell back into the chair. But this time, the chair couldn't hold his weight. He fell into the pool.

It was happening again. The family doctor and Mike were having those kinds of discussions that Philip mustn't hear. The doctor simply walked up to them and wanted to say something about a strange discovery in the autopsy report, but Mike said he'll see the doctor privately. He and the doctor walked into the office, and after some minutes, Mike could be heard yelling at the doctor.

"My brother drowned! He drowned! Guess who pushed him into the pool? His stupid son. I've always told him that the boy is mentally unstable, but he wouldn't listen. And here you are, telling me that there was another cause of death. What do you mean?"

"Sorry sir. I'm so sorry, I meant no disrespect. I'm just saying that the poison found in his system, which turned out to be the main cause of death was diluted with alcohol. It wasn't the inability to swim that killed him. Besides, why will he have a swimming pool in his house if he doesn't know how to swim?" The doctor stooped to explain his point.

"His son" Mike was bent on his point with feigned anger, pointing at the table while looking straight into the Doctor's eyes "pushed him into the water. How will he be able to manage the company after his father in the future without mental stability?"

"Mr Mike, we're not talking about the company here sir. We're talking about your brother's demise, the cause of death to be precise. Maybe I should give the report to his wife so that she'll know…"

"Don't do that" Mike cuts in "She's not in the right state of mind to know that her husband's death is more complicated than she knew"

"I thought you didn't agree to what was discovered in the autopsy report. Very well then, have it" He stretched the report papers over to Mike who took it and stuck it in his back pocket. "Another copy of the report remains here" the doctor said, but Mike was out of the office already.

Chapter 4

Extension plan...

"Listen Flora" Mike stated "I don't want to make a mistake here, and I'll not let you make any mistakes either."

"Ok. Just show me the autopsy report" Flora replied.

"I can't" He instantly retorted. "You know it's going to have Solomon's picture in the state of..." He gave a deep sigh "Look Flora, I know you loved your husband. But the thing is, I don't want you to get depressed only the more, okay?".

By now Flora, Solomon's wife was already sobbing. "And about Philip..." "Please, don't think I'm going to agree to what you suggested" Mrs. Bamford interrupted him.

"Look" Mike defied the interruption "I don't hate him, I just want the staff of my brother's company to accept him as a mentally sane personality in the futu..." Flora got up from the sofa and cuts in angrily.

"Are you saying my son is insane?" She said pointing a finger to the side of her head "He's only eleven years old, get that into your head Mike!"

"Flora please get my point. Philip pushed his own father into the swimming pool at that age and waited for him to drown before calling for help. Are you going to wait for him to be old enough to kill you too?"

"Mike" she replied with tears already welling up in her eyes "my boy will never do that"

"That's the point. I'm sure he hasn't apologized for what he did?" She shook her head amidst tears "That's because he doesn't see anything bad in such a grievous offence. He just needs to learn some things Flora; he needs to be somewhere he could be closely monitored. The staff of the company would appreciate this step towards restructuring Philip's mind, okay?"

Flora could no longer hold up. She bursts into tears " I'll be alone Mike, why are you doing this to me?" She sits on the ground crying, but Mike pulls her up " You have to be strong. Solomon won't be happy to see you this way".

Bob walked into the room with a swollen left cheekbone; he had obviously been involved in another fight, muttering inaudible words. Miss Howard followed closely behind, entered the room and stopped in front of Philip

"He was fighting at the dining hall. Take care of his wounds". She was about to squeeze the door knob when she turned around and fixed her gaze on Philip.

" That reminds me; I didn't see you in the dining hall today, why is that?" He tried to say something, but he just couldn't construct his words. "Philip" she walked closer to him "I wasn't the one who opted for another five years; it was your uncle that said the staff of your father's company suggested it. I tried to convince him that you're fine, but he insisted. He said your mother didn't want you to... you know what, I'm talking too much"

"My mother said what?" Philip wanted to hear more. "Tend his wounds" she pointed to Bob and left the room.

Bob. He is the son of a well-known polygamous billionaire, with of course many children too; 13 to be precise. So, of what use is an insane son amongst many children? Every time Philip looked at him, he's reminded of parents who care less about the children they bring to this world.

Your father is wealthy and resourceful, so why waste a good resource like this here? A few surgeries would do to adjust your mental structure, but your dad's indifferent. I've known this guy since I came here, and no matter how long I stay here, I know deep down within me that I'll leave him here. But does his father not care about him again? Come to think of it, I've never... His thoughts were interrupted when Terry walked into the room.

"Hey T" Philip called him as he fondly does. Bob said the same thing and kept repeating it, increasing his voice gradually and started laughing. "What happens now?" Terry asked Philip. "Honestly, I don't know.

Chapter 5

Escape plan...

Mrs. Bamford was putting on a black gown in remembrance of her husband's death. She was sober and she told the maid she wasn't going to see anyone to avoid disturbance as she ruminated on the drastic changes that had taken place since her husband died. Things haven't been the same obviously, but there was someone orchestrating all of this. Who could it be?

"Ma'am, someone's here to see you". Sarah, the head of all house staff came in her dainty apron that'll make anyone desire one. "Sarah, I told you I'm not interested in seeing anyone today as a ma..." "It isn't anyone" Mike walked into the room with a hand in his pocket and the other helping a chocolate bar into his mouth with Solomon's former guard, Tim tailing closely behind. He signaled Sarah to leave the room.

"Flora, I wanted to see you but you don't want to see anyone; you said it yourself. Why is that?"

"If everyone forgets, should it be you?

Should it be you that'll forget what happened on this day ten years ago?

" Flora replied, her patience burning out. Mike suddenly made a gesture suggesting a recalled memory "oh yes that's true. The staff of my brother's company will remember this, and it'll be well... remembered, whatever." He said, throwing his hands in the air. "So, tell me," Flora continued after maintaining eye contact with Mike for a while "what's this I'm hearing about the company's funds? We win contracts over and over again but we do not see the impact in the company. Please don't make me believe you're diverting the company's funds into your private acco..."

"Please stop it" Mike threw the unfinished chocolate bar at the wall. He hit the wooden table beside him, startling Flora. "I've had enough of this nonsense. What do you mean? You want to blame me for what the company is not enjoying? The only thing between you and Solomon is the lunatic you had for him. You need to see the way he's deteriorating in that mental home. Do you think I don't have the company's interest at heart by telling you not to visit him? I do not want to heighten your depressed state! As a matter of fact, I was the one who came here to see you, so don't ask me questions like I'm your puppet." Tears welled up Flora's eyes after hearing Mike's words. "I came here for a particular document; it's a proof of a completed project. We are meant to continually enjoy benefits because we didn't breach the agreement made. Tim, get the documents and meet me downstairs" Mike walked out of the room, leaving a shocked and teary-eyed Flora in it. When she was sure that Mike was downstairs, she grabbed Tim by his wrist. "You can see things for yourself, can't you? Is this what you'll pay my husband for all he did for you? He picked you from the gutter, remember?" Tim didn't say a word, he was quiet for seconds that seems like hours before he snatched himself from her grasp and left the house.

The day was over, and Philip could finally sleep after such a hectic day. Bob and Terry were fast asleep, so he laid down on his bed quietly and was drifting into sleep.

Suddenly, Bob began to knock the wall and cry, which he seldom did. Whenever this happened, it takes about thirty to forty-five minutes to calm him down. He had to be sung for like a toddler before he stops the act, which he must do willingly. Funnily enough, he was calmed in less than ten minutes. Uh...sweet relief.

He would finally sleep, so he thought. Just as he was drowning in the ocean of deep sleep, he was jolted back to consciousness by a knock on the door that went from being gentle to a very heavy knock, threatening to break the door. Miss Howard. "Get up, quick. Make sure you don't wake them. There are people waiting for you outside." He rushed out of the dormitory, sighted a car and saw faces he never expected to see. Tim and Mr. Callaghan were all smiling in the dark night upon seeing him. " I'm not sure you remember who I am" Mr. Callaghan started, extending his right hand for a hand shake. Philip shook his hand while trying to recall. "Mr. Call; that's what my dad called you. I still remember the long nose though." Philip said pointing to his very noticeable extra-long nose and giggled at his own joke. "Mr. Tim". "We've been plotting a perfect escape plan, I'm so sorry if it's taken too long. But first of, you should get rid of those clothes. And it's Tim, get rid of the 'Mr.' too. Let's go Sir". "I hope you brought clothes for two, because I won't leave without Terry."

Chapter 6

The Suspect...

You cannot imagine how long we've waited for this moment" Mr. Call emphasized. "Your uncle won't stop until he milks the company dry. He knows that I won't take that from him, that's why he brought one of his fraudulent friends to take my position and made me his assistant. As odd as this may seem, we have recovered some evidence we could use to pull him down." "I was surprised as well when I was told that he was the one who wanted me to stay another five years." Philip lamented.

"There's no time" Tim spoke up from the driver's seat "We have to take a step forward by the time the sun rises." "On the contrary" Philip had a second thought "I can't deny how tired I am, but my father's legacy is more important than a few hours of sleep." "Your call, Boss" Tim said as he briefly looked at Philip and returned his gaze to the road, but Mr. Call and Terry fixed their gaze on him. "Drop Mr. Callaghan at his house; Mike may suspect him once he finds out what has happened. It'll be safe if you don't have any idea where I am, but if I need anything, you're just a call away. For now, we're gonna pay the family Doctor's hospital a visit and search for our family's medical records. We must find the Doctor's copy of the autopsy report." Mr. Callaghan was getting off the car, Philip quickly held his wrist "Find my mother, tell her I'm in town." A nod was Mr. Callaghan's response. The trio headed for the hospital after dropping Mr. Callaghan off. Upon getting to the hospital, Tim stopped the car and sneered "The Doctor is still around". Terry cleared his throat and finally spoke up "Then we walk up to him make our request known. You have rights to your family medical reports because you're part of it." Tim expressed his doubts almost immediately "He may most likely not hand it over; he works for Mike now. We must make another plan, yours may no..." "No worries" Philip gave a wry smile "we'll work on the evidence we have; confirmation will come when we need it. Let's lodge in a hotel, I can't go home now, that'll be too easy." Tim started the ride.

"So, tell me" Philip continued through the ride "how did you not detect this? You should have seen this coming, how did you let this slide?" Tim shrugged "I'm sorry boss, I didn't know. I was worried about other things. I... " He shrugged again "he winked at me after giving your dad the drink, I thought it was a playful wink. I woke up in your father's office after it all happened, I didn't remember sleeping; so, I was made to believe all I heard. He cajoled me to work for him due to my loyalty to your dad. I started suspecting him when I discovered a secret room in his house." He paused. "It was full of chemicals Boss, chemicals" He glanced at Philip and focused on the road again. "Putting two and two together, I remember what the Doctor said about the autopsy report. A chemical, precisely one of your uncle's did it. At least, I was there when they were yelling at each other." He scoffed.

Terry heaved a sigh of relief and collapsed on the bed when they got to their booked hotel room. He started snoring almost immediately. Tim stood by the door. "I'll be awake Boss, I'll have to wa..." A knock on the door stopped the discussion. Tim pulled his gun out from his back and pointed it to the door. He opened the door gently, to find Dr. Wilson standing in the door way. His hands went straight into the air upon sighting the gun. "I'm only here to help. I saw your car outside the hospital through my window. I know I've been working for Mike for years now, but if for any reason he is involved in Solomon's death, I would do anything to fish him out. I'll do everything and contribute anything to find out who is responsible for the death of your father." He lowered a hand which was already shaky and sweaty, with the ten-year-old autopsy report in it. "Well, well well" Philip gave a wide grin "you had been following us. My allies grow by the hour." The Doctor walked into the room and handed the paper over to Philip "I'll stay here with you; we'll go to the company tomorrow; it's time to take what's yours. If we can nail him down with this, then he doesn't have a way of escape from every other mess he's gotten himself into." As he laid to rest, Philip had a childish excitement in him. Things are beginning to take shape.

Chapter 7

The Recovery...

Mr. Callaghan took his time in getting to work, knowing that the tide had turned. Besides, he had to work according to Philip's plan. So yeah, taking his time was part of it. He walked into his former office with both hands in his pocket

"Hello John. You're sitting at the wrong place" he smiled.

"Callaghan, have you forgotten who I am? You should regard me in a more respectful way!" He barked

"What way? If I may ask."

"As your Boss! Have you lost your manners?" He yelled more, attracting the attention of other staff.

"If you're truly my boss, you don't have to say it. I'll naturally respect you if you deserve it. And for the manners, a person with good manners won't be a fraudster." He smiled still. By now, everyone was around the office, trying to catch a glimpse of what was happening.

"I think I'm done with you already. Your time here is up. You're fired!" John was visibly angry now.

"Nope, he can't be fired just yet" a voice answered from a distance.

"Why?" John snarled angrily.

"Because I just promoted him. And he's right, you're sitting in his office" the voice replied again.

His anger had become confusion "What are you saying Mike?"

"I'm not Mike. I'm Philip, and I'm here to take what is mine" Philip, Tim, Dr. Wilson, Terry and Flora walked into the building.

"So you've planned a petty coup, right? John stammers, scratching the back of his head. A look of panic on his face, but he tries to laugh it off. Mike came out of the bathroom to see a scene playing out in the main hall of the company.

"What's going on here? Everyone back to w..." Mike was startled on sighting Philip and his followers. "How did you get here?"

"I walked right in. You?" Philip was relaxed.

"What do you mean?"

"Sorry for the questions but, we're playing sides here. So tell me, on whose side are you?" Philip had his hands in his pockets.

"I'm your family, your father's only brother"

"I honestly don't understand you Sir. I'll need you to throw more-light sir."

"I'm your uncle!"

Philip walked up to him and tucked at his sleeves. "My uncle. My uncle who killed my father using Hem lock to poison his whiskey." By now, all the staff of the company were in the hall. "My uncle who locked me up in a mental home for ten years and lied to my mother and everybody that my condition was deteriorating. My father's brother who made sure to pocket all the gain my father's company offered. My Uncle, who's aim is to eat up all my father built for decades!" Philip held his suit tight, obviously vibrating with anger. Mike quickly pulled out of his grasp looked out of the window. What he saw drained color from his face. Security agents had surrounded the building. Philip, with a devilish smile made his way to his uncle again, whose confusion had obviously risen to its peak. He wrapped his arms around Mike "Don't worry, you'll be just fine. I'll make sure you're not killed. You'll live the rest of your life in regret of all your actions." He said with passion in his voice.

Philip slowly walked into his father's office and sat down. He looked at everyone with a smile of accomplishment and slight disappointment. Then the applause started. Terry started the applause, then his mother. All the staff joined in, and the sound of people clapping could be heard halfway down the street.

About the Author

Adegboye Samuel is a great writer. He has been writing since he was in high school. While studying he has written a lot of articles that have blessed lives; his storyline ranges from Fictions to Christian piece of literature, fairy tales and poet. He also has educational publication like books and video tutorials. He is a lover of God and believers.

Acknowledgements

First of all, my appreciation goes to God, Almighty for the opportunity to collate this manuscript. I am grateful to number of friends, colleagues, and co-members in encouraging and supporting me to start the work, persevere with it, and finally to publish it.

THANKS FOR READING

www.ingramcontent.com/pod-product-compliance
Lightning Source LLC
Chambersburg PA
CBHW060357130626
46553CB00003B/1277